SHOW YOUR SELF: AUTHENTIC COMPASSIONATE LEADERSHIP

Janine E. Janosky, Ph.D.

AugustSolutionsGroup LLC

http://augustsolutionsgroup.com

Text Copyright @ 2017

By Janine E. Janosky

All rights reserved.

Show Your Self: Authentic and Compassionate Leadership

It is quite interesting that frequently the things that come to us as we least expect them are those that are most meaningful in our lives. I would imagine that you have experienced this, as I have. About ten years ago, I was waiting for an event to begin, a new staff orientation. This was one of those events that we all attend a number of times in our professional careers. We attend as leaders welcoming new staff, and we attend as new staff being welcomed by leaders. A welcoming to new people joining the organization; becoming acquainted with those who are joining us as well as having those be more acquainted with the institution or organization they have joined. As I was listening to the event speakers and preparing my remarks, I realized that we, as leaders who are being called upon to stand and give thoughts to our new colleagues, are at a crossroads decision. And, in those moments when I was preparing my remarks, I reflected – Do I do what is the perfunctory thing to do, which is to echo that this is a great place to work and we are pleased that they are now our colleagues? Do I echo agreed-upon talking points of the joys of working here, or do I perhaps do something more authentic? Is this the time to share some of who I am, what I am about, and how I made the decision to join this institution, including what I personally have given and gained from being here? What will be the benefits and the opportunities for them while they are here, specifically for their professional and personal growth as well as their opportunities to positively impact the institution and their personal growth? This is not really a complete sentence. You might want to make it a run-on from the previous sentence. It is always especially interesting to illuminate what the expectations of a leader are and what they need to do to share those expectations. And, as I reflected and prepared, I knew I was going to be called on as the third speaker. There were four institutional leaders to give remarks. I thought to myself, what would be the best approach, not only for those who are joining us here, but what would be the best approach for me to share myself as an authentic leader and to be authentic to myself as to who I am? So, I stood up and said – "What are the three tenets that guide all of my decision-making, whether I am considering engaging in a relationship or I am considering joining an employer or when I am considering whether I should leave an employer?" So that is exactly what I did. I did the thing that revealed who I am, and chose not to echo the agreed-upon talking points. I revealed things that perhaps our new colleagues should consider. Is the job really a paycheck or is it something more? Is it an opportunity to give of ourselves, to showcase and apply our strengths, to grow as a person, and make a difference in the world? Yes, if a job is a paycheck, it does have that benefit too, but, really, what are we all about? Are we about trying to make the world a better place? Are we about sharing our humanity and about enjoying the humanity of others? So, in that vein, I talked about the tenets for my life that drive my decision-making and leadership. These three tenets, for me, are: What should I be involved in and perhaps, equally as important, when should I stop being involved with something, and when should I say it is time for me to move on to the next, whatever that next might be? So, what are those three tenets?

Tenet One: Value for Who You Are

Tenet One is the start, a non-negotiable requirement. If Tenet One is not present, there should not be a consideration of moving on to Tenet Two or Tenet Three. If we think about many of the challenges in our professional and personal lives as well as the world today, these challenges are really related to this first tenet. The first tenet is a respect and understanding for who I am and also what I am. As I think about engaging in an employment situation, in a professional or personal relationship, in a community endeavor, or if I think about my leadership style, am I being welcomed and respected for who I am and the skill set that I bring, namely, what I am or am not? If this welcoming and respect is not present, the employment situation or leadership position, the personal or professional relationship, or the community endeavor, is not one where I should engage. It is not a place where I need to be. I ask the same of me when I reach to engage another. Do I respect whom I will be working with? Do I respect and value the skill sets from all of the individuals involved? Some of that exercise is a learning experience. We learn the value of each and every skill set, but it actually is a respect and an understanding issue. So, the first tenet is, when I think about engaging either in an employment situation, in a leadership position, in a relationship, working with a community, or any endeavor, the number one question is – will who I am and what I am be respected and valued, and, equally so, will I respect and value all others and do the same for them? Once we assure and secure this first tenet, then we can move on to the other two tenets. These tenets are so crucial as we engage with others and as we think about how it is that we choose to spend our time, choose to give to the world, choose to express our humanity, and choose to work with others as they express their humanity. Why is tenet one a crucial and non-negotiable requirement? As we serve as leaders, in our professional and personal lives, leading from a position of who we are and what we are is paramount. Leading as who we are and what we are is leading as our authentic self. By respecting and valuing each and every person, we are then in a trust position to express and bring a lens of our authenticity. As we work through respect and value for each person, our lens is a lens of compassion.

What are the final two tenets? When I spoke that day, I thought about the first tenet and how crucial it was for me as the foundation anchor when I was making the decision to join that institution. Did I feel who I was would be valued and respected? And did I feel that the work set or the skill set that I possessed was valued and respected? Equally so, as I require this value and respect of others, it is imperative that I also give these to others. If the answer is yes to this first tenet, we can move on to the next two tenets. Why is this so important? If we do not act from our authentic self, our opportunity to act from our strengths or skill set is not likely. As we feel valued for who and what we are, our ability and the likelihood of expressing our authentic self is increased. If not our authentic self, who then is present each day? Let us have a deep-dive into the first tenet, including leadership and specifically authenticity or authentic leadership with the lens of compassion. Paramount to authenticity is compassion, and we will deep-dive there too. As we enter this deep-dive, we will include Tenet Two and Tenet Three.

Tenet One: Value for Who You Are

Tenet Two: Making a Positive Difference

Tenet Three: Continuing to Grow

Leadership: Being a Leader

Broadly and historically, there are two long-held schools concerning leadership, with both sides citing history as their proof of sole effectiveness. One school holds that leaders are born, and the other holds that leaders are products of their environment. Which school is accurate, or are they both accurate? Does it matter if you suddenly find yourself in a leadership role? Some considerations follow when reflecting upon this bifurcation. The genetic or dynastic school holds that leaders are born, either due to genetic make-up or by their position in a dynastic situation. Born leaders, i.e., those who men and women follow willingly, are men like Julius Casar, Alexander, Charles 12th of Sweden, Churchill, Kennedy, and Roosevelt. The proponents of this school hold that the leader's DNA and consequently situation of birth provide them to be natural leaders. The chance school or environment school of leadership holds confident that leaders are products of the environment, as being shaped through their environment to fit into a role for which they are conditioned. Napoleon represents an example. Many chance school leaders rose to become leaders when the environment provided a particular set of optimal conditions for their emergence as a leader. As a leader who emerges as a chance leader through a sudden role position, what do you do? How do you become an effective leader? And what is an effective leader? One might argue that the definition of an effective leader is a value judgment, however, an effective leader is one whom those we lead will follow willingly, demonstrate respect, and trust. An effective leader leads followers to the goal of overall betterment of the current situation and is a supporter and an advocate of those who follow.

Crucial to becoming an effective leader is to identify and implement a system of goal fulfillment. The system of goal fulfillment would focus your trajectory for effectiveness by strengthening your values and qualities. A good leader must, first of all, know where and how he is leading. This system of goal fulfillment does not consist solely tactics to meet objectives; it is a system based on compassion, authenticity, respect, and values.

An effective leader must embody those qualities which he expects in others. As presented in Tenet One, as a leader, you show by example and expect the same of others—the value of who you are. Leadership is a rare commodity, as there are few leaders and many followers. Leadership from a focus of authenticity and compassion is a lens of leadership aligned with humanity and humility. This entails being direct and honest with yourself and those who follow you. Respect, trust, and admiration come from these two qualities when embodied by a leader.

An effective leader builds relationships with all colleagues, employees, managers, corporate officers... everyone. This skill is typically more than that referenced as 'networking' in the business world, a term that suggests business relationships are built only with those who can give something in return. An authentic compassionate leader expands the typical networking, moving beyond a transactional relationship. Instead of a transactional frame, these relationships of authentic compassionate leadership are focused on aligned visions and goals, including personal and professional goal fulfillment. Through authentic compassionate leadership, an effective leader works on the understanding that individuals and teams are more likely to collaborate and positively perform with a kind, caring, and honest person than they are one that seems only to have relationships when it is only the leader that has to gain from the relationship. An effective leader leads by example. One way that an effective leader demonstrates this quality is through the willingness to join their followers on tasks wherever it is necessary. Followers who see leaders joining in whenever and wherever necessary are usually more willing to go the extra mile themselves.

An effective leader helps develop skills in others, skills that they would want to develop and serve them well in their current position. These leaders provide extra training for those recognized as having a talent or an interest for certain areas. They promote these individuals to others in the organization. As a correlate, effective leaders notice when others are struggling and help them in a way the "student" can understand. Leaders know how to develop teams and they know how to motivate those teams to work together well. Building a team is an invaluable skill, and an effective leader knows how to develop a team that is based on trust, respect, and honesty. An effective leader gives credit to the team for successes and takes responsibility for challenges or unmet goals.

Leadership, A Sacred Responsibility

At the highest reaches of leadership, executive leadership, there is an attitude of profound and sacred responsibility. Great leaders view wisdom, courage, self-sacrifice, and strength of character as responsibilities of leadership, and set out to meet those responsibilities. For these leaders, every opportunity for leadership can properly be understood as containing a high potentiality, one that is realized through the quality of engagement that the leader brings to the position. Becoming and being a leader means you will have to become and be authentic, showing your true self.

What Leadership Entails

As with all things in life, successful leadership requires careful planning, consistent attendance, full participation, and precise results measurement. But to truly be successful as an effective leader, more is needed than just consistently attending events, meetings, and participation. Everyone values those who give their time and wisdom to ensure the success of the group. Giving your day in a purposeful way will yield the path toward results. A leader considers seeking opportunities to serve where their involvement will make the biggest impact for the group as well as for the leader and the organization or institution. Leadership must be consistent, demonstrating skills, enthusiasm, humanity, and humility to motivate and influence the group to remain on task, on time, on purpose, and ongoing.

Authentic compassionate leadership calls for humanity and humility. While as a leader you may be the captain of your team, leadership requires a servant mentality. To lead is to serve others. Bringing all your talent and skills is necessary; however, it is important to resist the temptation to be overbearing or perceive yourself as the only one with pertinent knowledge or the expert. Others are serving as well, and because of their service as well as service from the leader, authentic empathy and compassion is a strong leadership skill and frame. As Tenet One, a leader values each member of the team for who they are and what they are including their skill sets.

What is Your Claim to Being a Leader?

As Tenet One, one point of inception must be a value for who you are and what you are. This entails a clarity for you in self-knowledge of who you are and what you are, including your leadership skills and strengths. While many individuals ascend to and serve in a variety of positions of leadership, it often appears that some seem to be unfocused and unsure about their reasons for leading, as well as what they hope to accomplish in their positions. It is far easier to state that you believe you should be a leader than to demonstrate clearly why you should be doing so. Therefore, objectively looking at a combination of what an individual hopes to do, pledges to attempt, and in fact, accomplishes is crucial. Always consider, for yourself as a leader and for those who you follow you, what is your claim to being a leader?

- Leading must never be merely haphazard or undirected in practice. Rather, it must begin and be based on following one's authenticity to assure doing the right thing on a consistent basis. It is invariably not only an attitude, but rather a focus on providing a clarity of purpose, and a total and complete effort to do your best all the time.
- The emphasis of an effective leader must be on doing everything in a way as to enrich the lives and experiences of followers and constituents in a manner that enhances the organization and the greater benefit.
- Effective leaders invariably proceed with an actual and positive can-do attitude. However, even when

that is the case, unless it is accompanied by having developed a superior skill set and ability to address the needs of the group, far less than desirable effects are reached. Indeed, leading means maintaining a positive attitude and focus.

- The highest goals should be impactful and essential. The first goals are to beneficial for the organization as a whole. Staying steady to persist and persevere rather than succumb to challenges and become overwhelmed or diverted, for a meaningful determination, is paramount.

- Leading is not about the individual in the position, but rather the leader's desire and ability to conceive of and do whatever best meets the needs of the group. Therefore, an effective leader must possess impactful and consistent empathy and compassion. It will increase the involvement of the followers, because it will encourage them to care more and develop a caring and emotional connection.

- One can never claim to be an effective leader unless one maintains relevance by addressing present and future needs, being rational in evaluations and understandings, conveying essential rationale in an open and clear manner, and effectively relating to everyone involved.

To Being a Leader

The following are five consideration requirements to being an effective authentic leader, for successful individuals and team impact and growth:

- **Act**

A leader is a leader by title, though an effective leader is a leader by action. This does not preclude engaging with your followers regarding tactics or more, though, ultimately, an effective leader moves to action.

- **Know**

Your task as a leader is to lead your followers responsibly and effectively. To do this, you have to know your followers, knowing the strengths of each person as well as of the team, what they find interesting, their challenges, and more. This is directly aligned with Tenet One, including leading through the lens of compassion.

- **Structure**

Once you know your followers, the qualities of your followers and of your teams, this drives your guidance, direction, and motivation. With this known information, the project-specific structure, the operations, and the infrastructure can be developed and implemented. Task assignments of team deployment follow structuring.

- **Engage**

Allowing followers and other people to contribute, ask questions, and give feedback to the entire process provides for an open leadership, while building and maintaining trust. As everyone feels like they are equally contributing to the process, or are invited to contribute, more commitment and success will be gained. An effective leader makes sure that everyone contributes something, seeing their role as crucial to the success of the whole.

- **Evaluate**

A means for assuring individual and team growth is to assess and evaluate. These evaluations are best as broadly focused on not only the outcomes of goals met, but also the process of working together, lessons learned, skill development, and so forth.

Leaders Lead From Vision

An effective leader looks into the future and imagines and visions. This becomes the core of a strategic vision and is the foundation for moving the company or organization into the future. The strategic vision becomes the centerpiece of the direction of the business and is the primary element around which the human capital or people and resources are organized. At lower levels of the organization, the strategic vision is translated into goals and tactics for business units, teams, and individuals. Leaders articulate that strategic vision. The role of leadership is to transfer and translate the strategic vision through a shared vision for all and to the workings of the organization so that it becomes actionable. This process is annunciated by communicating that vision; leaders share, explain, enroll, persuade, and use every communication tool, personal and organizational, to spread the word, to achieve shared understanding and commitment. They build purpose, direction, and focus. They work to detail the action flowing from the vision, and they add substance and detail. An effective leader inspires others by embodying the idea; they provide someone and something around which others can organize themselves and their thoughts and efforts. They work to create order and coherence, to build a meaningful whole, a means for people and resources to meet the challenges and opportunities contained within the strategic vision. They influence their followers and others to aim higher, perform better, and deliver more. Leaders influence others to turn the vision into reality. They help build a map through the complexity and confusion and chart their way through challenges. They work to create the culture that is needed for achieving the vision. They build and enforce networks of accountability that are critical to achieving the vision. They recollect the past and envision the future; they stand with one foot in the present and the other in the future. They seek to describe, in a meaningful way, the movement from the past into the present, and the present into the future. Effective leaders wrestle with the complexity of time, the big picture, and the details, and they work to arrive at an integrated and coherent conception that can be communicated to all relevant and interested parties. They describe purpose, values, and vision. All of this applies to leaders in all industries for all sizes of businesses, the difference being only in scope and complexity.

Authentic Leadership or Being An Authentic Leader?

Authentic is defined as "not copied or false", "genuine", and "verified". Likewise, genuine is defined as "free from pretense or hypocrisy", "sincere", and "a genuine person". Through this lens, leadership is about being honest and genuine and not being hypocritical or false. The possible refinement on leadership might be in order. Leadership is a position or a title that you hold. You may have the title because you have some expertise or skills that the business or team needs. If we needed to build a bridge, the person given the leadership role is the person that has the specific skills related to building that bridge. We would work under their leadership because they have the skills needed for this job that needs to be done. Authentic leadership can mean having the authentic skills or certain skills required to get the task done.

Being a leader is something different. There is a difference between the person who has particular expertise and so is given a leadership role and the person who is a leader because they can lead. The difference between being a leader and having leadership is the word 'being.' A leader that is genuine or authentic is the leader who has the ability to lead, however, not purely based on skills or knowledge but on who he or she is as a person. In other words, it is a part of their 'being'. So, the words, "free from pretense or hypocrisy" and "not being hypocritical or false" are paramount to genuine leadership. We are talking about a person that has developed their 'being' in a way that makes them a leader of individuals. *Being a leader is about who we are.* So, being a leader is about expressing your ability of being a leader. And that is a major challenge. As we might consider an engineer, we might call the engineer a leader in their profession when they have successfully lead the building of a functional bridge. Verification is clear and validation is easy to be established. Many people think that because they have excellent skills or knowledge, this is all that is needed to be a leader. Since the engineer demonstrated the skill in successfully leading the building of the bridge, then they must be a leader. In truth, their excellent skills and knowledge only validate their ability to hold a leadership role, but ultimately, they may not be the leader. Authentic leadership is about being. "A leader is most effective when people barely know he exists. When his work is done, his aim fulfilled, his troops will feel they did it themselves." - Lao Tzu

What is Authenticity?

Recently, authentic leadership has emerged as the 'gold standard' of leadership, as proclaimed in 2015 by the *Harvard Business Review*. Gaining popularity in the business world, especially following the ethical considerations raised during the most recent global financial crisis, authentic leadership is based on honesty, sincerity, and integrity. It is a leadership model in which the motivation for leadership is by a purpose larger than oneself rather than self-interest. The leader works to build trust by acting in alignment with their solid values.

As leaders encounter entirely new challenges and responsibilities, they realize that they have the personal strengths and personal resources to meet these challenges. For example, some first-time leaders ultimately learn that they have a gift for expressing and leading through inspiration of others. Others find that they are especially talented at strengthening and leading through motivations and values. Each time you make an impact as a leader—whether it is shaping your unit's or institution's culture in positive ways, helping someone master a new task, or assembling a high performing team—leaders expand their abilities. They become more seasoned, experienced, and confident, and have a sharper awareness of their own strengths and personal resources. Not only do leaders learn more about themselves as they progress in a leadership role, they also learn more about organizational life and the value in each and every skill set. Leaders continuously learn as stated through Tenet Three, and live Tenet One.

The command and control techniques as a leadership model are increasingly ineffective. Today's leaders must be forward-thinking, possess moral courage, and be skilled in the art of diplomacy. The changing structure of organizations and institutions, the growth of alliances or collaborations between and among organizations, and the changing nature of work itself call for new approaches to leadership. Authentic leadership has less to do with formal authority and the power to control, and more to do with using situational, strategic, and ethical leadership skills to influence individuals who may not report to you, aligned with an overarching vision and purpose.

Leadership is not just about logic and reason. Logic and reason have their place; however, there is much more. Acknowledging that it is not all rational is a major step toward accepting that there is something more important – the feelings, emotions, and personal visions and goals of individuals. Leaders need to understand that at the heart of their leadership is working the ability to influence and advance the best of each and every individual. Leaders learn and live Tenet One.

To gain and keep the commitment of followers, the relationship between the leader and follower has to be nurtured. Leadership is a relationship between those who aspire to lead and those who choose to follow. Diplomacy in leadership requires that we not only know and understand our own emotions, but also learn how to recognize other people's emotions as well. What a leader achieves now depends on the people they are leading, and the best way to succeed is to influence others to give their best. The job of a leader is to achieve a vision via achieving goals – that is the end; leading people is the means.

Authenticity is the quality or condition of being trustworthy or genuine. It can be described as being and acting from the true self without masks and personas. Learning about yourself is perhaps the single most important outcome of a powerful leadership and follower experience. Self-awareness can lead to an ever-increasing authenticity which, in turn, leads to powerful leadership abilities. Authenticity is not about 'accept me for what I am'; authentic leaders are self-aware, willingness to adapt and change, and 'be who they are in service to others.' Education should be a powerful process of increasing self-awareness, of coming to know yourself and of learning the intrinsic value of who you are as a human being, and then understanding the need for constant change, personal growth, and learning.

Someone who is authentic will speak and act congruently, and their words and gestures, tone, and volume will all match the content of what they are saying. They will speak and act in ways that reveal their true beliefs, views, opinions, and emotions even when this might conflict with those of whom they are communicating.

Authenticity is hard to develop and even harder to coach. Authenticity is a way of "being" as a leader, rather than what you do as a leader. Responsibility for authenticity, then, belongs to the leader. Through a combination of introspection and discipline, leaders find their authentic voice and amplify it so that it can be understood by their followers.

One of the most difficult tasks for those who would measure and evaluate leadership is the task of dissecting the elements that comprise leadership. One way to look at these elements is to suggest that a leader has various skills, exercises a distinctive style, and, still more elusive, has various qualities that may be annunciated. By skills, one typically looks to the capacity to do something well, something that is learnable and can be improved, such as speaking or negotiating or planning. Most leaders need to have technical skills such as writing well; human relations skills such as empathy; the capacity to supervise, inspire, and build coalitions; and also what might be called conceptual skills – the capacity to play with ideas, shrewdly seek advice, and forge grand strategy. Skills can be examined and assessed. Skills can be taught. And skills plainly comprise an important part of leadership capabilities. These skills alone, however, cannot guarantee success.

A way of being as a leader, some consider as a leadership trait, or considered by some as a skill, admired, encouraged, and effective is authenticity. Often, rather than authenticity, it feels easier to hide behind whatever cover the leader has created; although it is comfortable, it is not ultimately rewarding and effective. For your consideration, do I value others more for how honest they are or how honest they appear?

Use of honesty includes these capabilities:

Directness that is candid and comfortable.

Disclosure concerning issues of import.

Assessment that is meaningful, actionable, and compassionate.

Expression of one's own genuine thoughts.

Discussion of uncomfortable, though performance critical, topics.

Effective leadership too must come from deeply felt impulses: the source of authenticity. Leadership is more than delegating or giving orders. The other-giving way of leadership is the lowest form of leadership, and it is leadership that most lends itself to the afflictive mask or non-authenticity. A leader may be successful in garnering a response to an order, especially if compensation is involved, but only when you establish deep, human, emotional connections with people will they go out of their way to accomplish the often challenging, difficult tasks needed to garner exceptional results. If you are not authentic, you are less likely to establish those connections. Establishing those connections flows from empathy and compassion.

There are two primary paths to being authentic: the inner path and the outer path. Before you can be authentic, you must BE authentic. This seeming tautology points to a deep truth about authenticity; it is not only a state of awareness, it is a state of being. The showing of your self is being authentic. There has been much written about getting in touch with your feelings and living life from this awareness. Two primary questions are drivers: (1) Are you prepared to do your job; i.e., do you have the skills, experience, and knowledge to be in your position? (2) Why are you here?

Answering both of these questions is crucial. These two are directly aligned with Tenet One. The answer to the second question is the heart of authenticity. The answer should be tied to a leader's drive: as we work to achieve the vision, our goals, and the needed results, all will grow professionally and personally. This is Tenet Three. Each day, as we generate our motivation for our day by re-committing to the leadership drive, our motivation as a leader is: today, I will work on every interaction with every person to achieve results while helping them grow professionally in their job skills and their personal goals. your authenticity will develop in the crucible of the daily, inner commitment. This leads to an important part of authenticity: Your authenticity is of limited value in leadership terms unless it is communicated. The vehicles of communication is the leadership drive.

The Value of Authenticity

When you are working for a leader who is authentic, what is your experience? You experience their honesty; however, you may not always know how it will appear. There is a positivity that accompanies that ambiguity... assurance. If you know you work for someone who will be honest, there is assurance in knowing that however uncomfortable the message, it will be delivered with honesty through compassion. You will not need to be concerned about hearing it from someone else or leaving the conversation confused...you will know what you need to know. There are enough misunderstandings that happen unintentionally. The more we can minimize intentional misinterpretations, the better. If we want to grow as leaders or followers, we have to be willing to have uncomfortable conversations. Uncomfortable conversations are driven through authenticity.

Leadership depends on an ability to call forth authentic action in response to the issues it identifies. As you recognize the issue accurately, you still must respond accurately, authentically, and appropriately. The following three questions are drivers to lead you to be an authentic leader:

What am I doing that feels contrary to who I actually am?

What part of me and my experience would my team benefit from knowing?

What is one thing I can do now that will help me to show more of my true self to my team?

Strategies to Becoming an Authentic Leader

It is difficult, and perhaps not possible to be an authentic leader, unless you are your own person or true self. Authentic leadership requires a leader to show your self. Trying to imitate someone else or being too responsive to the expectations of others is not conducive to being an authentic leader. You must be yourself. People will see your strengths and want to follow someone who is true and genuine. Develop your own unique leadership style. Be consistent with your own personality.

Understand and live your purpose. If you lack purpose and direction in leading, why would anyone want to follow you? In order to find your purpose, you must first understand yourself. What are you passionate about? Are there any underlying motivations? What excites your soul? Authentic leaders are defined by values and character, and integrity is the one value that is required. If others cannot trust you, why would they follow you? If your followers do not know you, why would they follow you? There will be situations in which your values are challenged, and you must make tough decisions in the context of your values. Lead with your heart; lead through compassion for everyone. The capacity to develop close and genuine relationships is a mark of an authentic leader. As a leader might have a detached style of leadership and cannot or will not connect with the people you lead, it will be difficult to be effective. It is your life experience that opens up your heart to have compassion for the most difficult challenges people have along life's journey. This is authentic leadership.

Self-discipline is a critical quality of an authentic leader. Without self-discipline, it is difficult for a leader to gain respect of the people whom you lead. If a leader has good values but not the self-discipline to put them into action, they lose trust. Also, know that none of us are perfect, so when we fall short, it is important to admit our errors and demonstrate resilence. This hold for a leader, too. In addition to admitting to errors and demonstrating resilence, as an authentic leader, you must practice consistency and self-discipline. Learn how to handle the pressure of leading. Becoming an authentic leader requires many years of hard work, some pain and suffering, and the wisdom that comes from experiencing life at the fullest. Paramount to self-discipline is building self-awareness. By understanding your leadership type and by taking an assessment to understand yourself; then, learn about your colleagues. By knowing who you are and who they are, a leader can create an environment in which followers are able to comfortably be themselves and create a common language where they understand one another. In this environment or culture, the balance allows followers to be completely who they are and also be aligned with the culture of the overall group.

Understanding your personal developmental perspective, such as complexity of thinking, emotional intelligence, and behavior, affords a leader the ability to internalize the perspective of many different levels. By understanding the primary perspective of your followers and meeting them where they are, you show the highest degree of respect and appreciation. Building resilience includes developing a strong sense of emotional intelligence. Emotional intelligence includes self-awareness and knowing your strengths and preferences. It also includes understanding others' strengths and preferences, and demonstrating the flexibility to respond to another's level appropriately. The golden rule of authentic leadership could be --- treat people as they need to be treated to perform at their best. Since we are all unique and have different expectations, treating others as you want to be treated exemplifies authenticity in a leadership role.

Developing situational analysis is the combination of understanding yourself and the organization or institution. By using situational analysis, you are able to understand the balance between your values and the needs of the organization and act in a manner that attends to your authenticity while balancing the organization's expectations and norms. This means you can read the situation quickly and respond accordingly. This does not mean you change your innate preference or act in a way that is not genuine, but rather, in many cases, learn to expand your repertoire of skills and behaviors. Aligning leadership behavior means behaving in a manner that is authentic to you and appropriate to the organization and situations in which you find yourself. To do this well, it means you need access to a broad range of behaviors and have the skills referenced in situational analysis to diagnose the organization's needs and your authentic style, and have the skills to balance both. By expanding your abilities, you can be agile while being authentic.

Authentic leadership requires acting in alignment with your values. How consistently do your actions follow your words? Being present and practicing mindfulness or another practice will help you attune into how well you are connecting with followers and aid in assessing your alignment with your values. Authentic leaders are also known for being genuine and real. They connect and build rapport with others by learning about them and finding common ground to reveal their approachability. This does not mean uncontrolled expression or being transparent about what you are thinking and feeling at all times, which may result in losing credibility or effectiveness. Also, it does not open an excuse for bad behavior under the guise of authenticity. Authentic leaders should match their behavior to the context. This involves selective self-disclosure and vulnerability based on what is appropriate for a particular situation. Use your judgment to adjust your style or reveal different, but true, facets of your personality depending on the circumstances and what would benefit your followers.

Living from a position of authenticity requires practice to become comfortable with being authentic and skilled at adapting your leadership style to find the balance between demonstrating authority and approachability. Effective leaders understand that their reputation for authenticity needs to be earned and carefully managed. It is important to recognize that we are all growing and learning, so your authentic self will also evolve over time. As authentic leaders, we need to explore and choose effective styles, behaviors, and tactics, and then integrate what works for us into our own leadership style. This calls for us to take time to reflect and process our leadership experiences. Being an authentic leader can be challenging but also meaningful and rewarding for both you and those you lead.

Tenet Two: Making a Positive Difference

From and through our authentic self, we are in a position to express and lead through who and what we are. The second tenet is the opportunity to make a difference through your leadership. Serving as an authentic compassionate leader calls for the opportunity and need to make a positive difference or impact. Once tenet one is secured, the second tenet further drives the decision of where to lead, what to lead, and how long to lead.

Have you ever wondered why some people and organizations excel, even in difficult times? Faced with unprecedented challenges, some people and organizations fail, others simply survive, but a few grow and even prosper. What makes the difference? In our professional and personal lives, most of us want to strive to make a positive difference. Do we see making a difference as an opportunity? Making a difference differs from making a change. To make a positive difference, change must result in a positive benefit for everyone or, at best, the majority involved. Leading successful change at work and in our lives is a choice. Leaders who frame change as opportunity ultimately find ways to succeed. How do leader's and entire organizations create a mindset or culture toward making a difference? Intentionally or intuitively, they create the conditions for people to embrace change as a positive challenge. Making a difference for a positive impact at work and in your life are based on the following concepts:

Build Common Vision and Purpose – Why Change

Determine the Strategy and Clarify the Direction – What to Change

Identify Infrastructure and Develop Capacity – We Can Change

Inspire Collaboration and Teamwork – We Want to Change

These are not common practice; however, they are logical and provide a structure. Conversely, in order to make a difference for the better, you need to address "the why," "the what", and "the how." How includes ability (We can make a difference.) and motivation (We want to make a difference.). For a change to succeed and to be sustainable, it needs to show evidence of success early on; orchestrating quick and early wins provides much needed credibility and motivation. The approach for making a difference, through engagement and process, is as important as what you are changing. Authenticity in your leadership, as well as the authenticity in the process, should drive the culture. In the process, the following keys could be beneficial.

Having an Impact: Leading and helping people directly reach their personal and professional goals.

Supporting a Positively-Focused Team: Supporting a team that is thriving and working to make a difference.

Fostering Community: Improving the work environment, physical and non-physical infrastructure, will have a positive impact.

Showing up Positively: How you choose to show up; be proactively positive in an authentic way.

Finding Meaning: Leading and acting from and through higher meaning, realizing and communicating the vision and the group and individual's contribution to meeting the vision.

The Compassionate Leader

When you think of leadership roles or talk of being a leader, the word compassion does not typically come to mind. Most people do not realize that compassion is one of those qualities that differentiates a good leader from a great leader. The typical leader has been conditioned to believe that they should put business before compassion, to rule with their minds and not their hearts. The conventional image the general populous has of an effective leader is someone who is decisive, tough, strong, result-driven, hard-nosed, and rational. Contrary, or perhaps congruent, to these images, effective leaders also possess the confidence, courage, and conviction to cultivate compassion and connectivity.

Most people still see compassion as a somewhat distant and self-sacrificing ideal. They consider it an unrealistic response of those that are naively sentimental or all too kind-hearted and are seen as too soft or diluting hard decisions when they should be stern and stoic and even ruthless in their approach to business. More businesses and organizations are now interested in a more compassionate style of leading, one that is from the heart and not entirely from the head. While this may seem like nothing more than human kindness, it makes practical business sense. Most employees do not perform well in an environment filled with negative emotions. A lot of productivity and performance problems lie in this emotion-filled area. Any leader who wants his or her followers to perform at their optimal best must first connect at the emotional level, and this connectivity is compassion. Although we may try to convince ourselves that there is no space for compassion and connection, the greatest and most effective leaders always make time for some compassion. They care about connecting with the people who follow them. They believe connectivity is the conduit for almost all they do, and compassion is the key to that connectivity. Compassionate leaders possess the innate ability to inspire people with hope, optimism, energy, and purpose. This is because they resonate and can empathize and connect with the people they lead. Even though a driven, directive, and coercive leadership style may motivate people in the short-term, the discord it sparks creates an environment filled with toxic emotions like anger, apathy, and anxiety and also could cause dramatic long-term damage such as a toxic workplace. Compassion and connectivity not only aid in bolstering emotional and social factors that help to create a vibrant working relationship, but they are also essential elements that help workers maintain emotional balance, build up their reserves of resilience, relieve leadership stress, insulate from the harmful effects of toxic emotions, and renew individuals and teams.

Compassionate Leaders in History

Before we continue, let us look at some of the leaders in history. And yes, some may be considered controversial; however, valuable lessons can be considered.

Napoleon Bonaparte: As you consider the layers of history, one leader, though considered by some as ruthless, is the French leader, Napoleon Bonaparte. Even though most of his decisions were quite controversial, he was also a leader who was in touch with his followers. Napoleon was once described as a leader who completed tasks that most people would consider beneath his role. Wherever was needed on the battlefield, he was there. A key lesson to learn from Napoleon is his willingness to join in the work with his followers. Even though he was an Emperor, he did not consider any job beneath him and was committed to the responsibility of completing the job. As a modern-day leader, this is a practice to embrace. His willingness to complete tasks meant for others made his men believe that he actually cared about the cause and their issues for the fighting. The practice here: learn to take part in the work of your followers. By adopting a hands-on approach, you will be able to connect with your followers on an individual and more intimate level. It also showcases your commitment to the cause that all of you are working toward which could bring about a more passionate work ethic from your employees.

Nelson Mandela: He is one of the most influential leaders in history. The life of Nelson Mandela is filled with countless lessons, all of which can be applied to human management and business leadership. One effective practice is his lifelong belief in learning. Mandela himself held degrees from multiple higher education institutions. To paraphrase one of his more popular quotes '…Education is the most powerful weapon that you have at your disposal to change the world.' One, and especially leaders, should not end their education with completing their formal studies. Part of what lifelong learning entails is a willingness to continue learning and growing from your experiences as well as the continuation of studies, both formal and informal. Education enriches us with a better understanding of people and ideas which, in turn, makes us better informed and wiser leaders. This is Tenet Three.

John F. Kennedy: This former United States president is a well-known leader. John F. Kennedy is examined mostly for his expansive thinking ability and for the constant high goals he wanted the citizens of America to achieve. President Kennedy had great machinations and was willing to set goals that other people would consider unachievable. Everyone can learn from Kennedy – from aspiring leaders to the ones already established in their respective fields. Learn to set hard to reach goals, stretch goals, that will challenge you and your followers. The greatest leaders do not seek out tasks that can easily be achieved. They seek out change as well as jobs that will revolutionize. To become an effective great leader, you need to start challenging your skill set and carry your followers to greatness.

Margaret Thatcher: Her famous nickname, "The Iron Lady", garnered all kinds of popularity for this controversial British Prime Minister. Regardless of her experiences, a constant throughout her career was her incredible resilience, part of what earned her the famous nickname. No matter how tough a challenge appeared, she was always able to rise to the occasion. The more difficult the problem, the more it seemed she rose to the occasion, and she appeared to thrive on it. Her leadership style was a reflection of her personality; she was a challenge-oriented individual with a strong sense of self and confidence. As a leader, one will frequently face adversities and challenges, and in those situations, strength and resilience are needed.

Mahatma Gandhi: Of all the leaders previously mentioned, none conjure up the image of compassion more than Mahatma Gandhi. He is considered one of the most compassionate and ethical leaders. He is known for the quote, "In a gentle way, you can shake the world." This quote was an indication of his desire to change the world and his belief that he could accomplish it through compassion. As a leader, Gandhi possessed the ability to step into the circumstances of others and gain a deeper understanding of the issue from their perspective. The capacity to have compassion and empathize with those around you is integral to the characteristics of a great authentic compassionate leader. With those qualities, you can connect more easily with those you lead and demonstrate to them that you care and are leading with compassion.

Overall, the leadership qualities exhibited by these leaders are ways of being an authentic compassionate leader. They include: doing what you have asked others to do, lifelong education, aspiring to achieve stretched goals, the advantage of being resilient, and, last but not least, the value of having compassion as a leader.

Building a Case for Compassion

Often, we experience an absence of compassionate leadership in the workplace. Fortunately, that is beginning to change. More organizations and businesses are starting to realize that caring for one another and embracing emotions do make for a safe, efficient, and effective workplace. They have realized that leaders also need to possess a high level of emotional intelligence. This growing interest in leading with feelings has paved the way forward in taking the next step of cultivating a more compassionate leader.

As organizations and businesses begin to shift to a more caring, emphatic, and emotionally intelligent style of leadership, some issues arise such as: What is compassion? What does being a compassionate leader entail? How does compassion align within the context of effective leadership? Can compassion be learned? Compassion in the workplace is beginning to be studied and there are emerging findings of benefits. In addition to the definitive observations, it appears that compassion:

- promotes empathy as an effective and connective leadership style
- calms the physiological effects of stress by calming body reactions
- helps to maintain emotional balance and manage disruptive moods
- insulates against the harmful effects of toxic emotions on the mind and the body
- opens one to other positive emotions like hope and optimism
- builds a reserve of resilience which is essential in handling setbacks

- increases well-being
- aids to renew and sustain the energy levels of leaders

Another benefit of cultivating compassion is that it contributes to other positive changes in how a leader leads, handles the stress and unavoidable toxicity of the job, and how he or she relates to others. This quality of compassion also allows leaders to exude less employee disapproval and, instead, show more concern, making them easier to approach. Reduced displays of toxic emotions like anxiety and anger create a calm and more emotionally balanced approach, and this increased understanding and empathy, in turn, increases the trust between followers and leaders. All of these are important qualities for authentic leadership.

The Components of Compassion

What are the elements of compassion? To answer this completely, we should not only rely on modern Western psychology, but also consider the venerable contributions of Eastern religion and practices, such as Buddhism. Compassion is considered one of the four main pillars of Buddhism. Frequently, the West tends to focus on emotional challenges rather than how to cultivate positive emotions particularly compassion.

To paraphrase the words of Lorne Ladner's The Lost Art of Compassion, we have been taught how to '...work with negative and often damaging emotions'; however, not in Western psychology has it offered one clear, well researched, and practical method that can be used to develop compassion. Although the East and the West have their differences in how they understand compassion, some of the essential components are common to both practices. These are:

- **Respect and Caring**

Compassion has been described as involving curiosity, caring, empathy, and respect toward other people. This belief is also echoed by the Dalai Lama who has defined it as "a mental attitude that is associated with a sense of responsibility, respect, and commitment."

- **Empathy**

The religion of Buddhism considers compassion a deep understanding of the emotional state of another, which is similar to the Western idea of empathy. Compassion makes us feel empathy. This is, of course, a slight reversal of the thought of the West which sees empathy as what allows us to connect with other people and makes it possible to feel compassion.

- **Selfless and Unconditional**

Both Eastern and Western tradition consider these conditions essential for compassion. Selfless and unconditional paractice is the ability to place the need of others before yours and not favor trade or expect something in return or give or withhold compassion. This practice holds whether one is considered as your friend or your foe. Compassion means selflessly giving of yourself. It does not expect or assume equal exchange or a tradeoff.

- **Committed Action**

Compassion is empathy and caring in action. It is a willingness to act out on those feelings. According to the Dalai Lama, genuine compassion is not only an emotional response but also a firm commitment that is characterized by action.

- **Beneficial to Others**

In Buddhism and Eastern philosophy, compassion is meant to alleviate suffering. In the West, compassion is about being benevolent with no thought of personal gain.

It can be difficult to feel true genuine compassion. It is usually when the relationship with the other party is one filled with positivity and positive emotions. It becomes much harder when such feelings are absent or when the relationship is tainted by dislike, envy, indifference, resentment, or other negative emotions. It is essential for every one of us, both leaders and followers, to act compassionately. We must first find this mental state of compassion inside of us, and then make our intentions for being compassionate clear. We can carry out compassionate acts which will result in good consequences, but if you were to delve deeper, why did you do it? Since compassion is a state of heart, it is difficult to measure or discern by a person's outward behavior. Behavior may easily be misconstrued as benevolent when the truth is that the motivations are selfish desires, rather than a genuine feeling of compassion and fear.

The Dilemma with Being a Compassionate Leader

The fundamental belief and thought behind compassion are a true connection in situations where people are suffering and being able to take action whenever and wherever possible to help alleviate some of that suffering. Because of how they act and what they do, compassionate leaders can create a positively energized and emotionally healthy workplace. They have a genuine care for the well-being of others and pay close attention to their needs which they place before their own. They are aware of how their feelings impact the mood of others. Compassionate leaders can connect with their followers through empathy and use this connection to keep in tune and in touch with the thoughts and feelings of others. They also use positive emotions to inspire others and reduce toxic emotions that demoralize and sow discord in the workplace.

Being a compassionate leader also comes with its own dilemma. A compassionate leader works to relieve the pain of others, but as a leader, one inevitable side effect of leading is creating pain or discordance. Creating pain comes with the territory of being a leader. It can be thought of creating disodance, the pain, the difference between where the performance of the organization or individual is now as compared to where the leader envisions or wants it to be. While leaders sometimes provide excitement and inspiration, leadership is also about pushing the limit, setting new directions, and making decisions that will not necessarily make the leaders popular with their followers. In fact, the leader is more often going to leave them feeling frustrated, angry, afraid, and disillusioned.

Effective or great leaders understand the dynamics of leaderships and usually take steps to minimize, mitigate, and dissipate some of the pain they generate. Toxic emotions and stress are two of the possible side effects of leading.

- Toxic emotions: If they remain in the body, they slowly create cracks in our defenses. Bursts of adrenaline gradually wear down the immune system which results in mental and physical ill-health.

- Leading Stress: Having to handle constant crises, making hard decisions, constantly being aware for the well-being of others can be draining. Your reserves of empathy, resonance, and connectivity can and will lessen, and even the most resonant leaders will slip into dissonance.

Toxic emotions and stress may result in a leader being dispirited, burnt out, abrupt, scratchy, and abrasive. And because human emotions are contagious, this sense of discord quickly spreads to those around us and will eventually permeate your organization or institution. The busier we are, the more stressed out we become which, in turn, causes us to lose our groundedness. We become off balance, and our energy, focus, and equilibrium start to wane. This causes us to become distant, and we lose any sense of connection which is essential for compassion and authenticity. Our focus begins to center more on us, on how tired we are, of how behind we are, and how much is demanded of us, all of which makes us more disconnected. Prolonged periods of dissonance will promote the spread of toxic behavior and negative emotions which spread easily to affect those you lead.

The Results of Practicing Compassion

To counter the toxic effects of dissonance, leaders need to cultivate behaviors and habits of the mind that relieve or at least dilute them. Before you can return to the state of resonance, you must renew yourself through a conscious process of physical and mental practices that inspire, reenergize, and can counter the effects of stress.

Behavior and Traits of a Compassionate Leader

There are professional and personal benefits of adopting a more compassionate style of leadership. There are behaviors and characteristics that make a compassionate leader and are an expansion of those described for authentic leadership, and these traits include:

- **Focus on Connection and Collaboration**

A compassionate leader demonstrates a people-first approach as well as follower-centeredness. They also showcase high levels of Emotional Intelligence and can regulate their own feelings and assist those they lead to perform the same. Compassionate leaders have a highly developed focus on the human or people aspect of leadership. They also showcase high levels of commitment and empathy that allows them to understand how their actions and decisions could affect those they lead. Compassionate leaders invest a lot of effort and time into their staff.

- **Flexibility and Adaptability**

Compassionate leaders are flexible and able to adapt to the environment they find themselves in which allows for tailor-made approaches to specific situations and followers. This allows for a more personalized and less standardized approach to leadership and solutions. Because of this, compassionate leaders can respond to a particular situation or person instead of using previously learned ways of responding, or using behavioral profiles that are most times influenced heavily by unhelpful cultural beliefs and assumptions of an organization. Compassion makes leadership less reactive and more thoughtful.

- **Balance and Self-Caring**

Every compassionate leader can demonstrate a capacity and understanding to look after themselves and then model this self-care to their followers. Compassionate leaders are balanced in whatever they do. They can look after themselves as well as others and are still able to attend to institutional or organizational drivers, targets, and goals. Compassionate leaders understand the value of encouraging, ensuring, and facilitating those that they lead to have a balance between work and life which engaging in practices they preach.

- **Enabling, Empowering, and Inclusive**

Compassionate leaders are all about empowering and enabling self-reflection and development. They deliver positive and constructive feedback that focuses on developing potential and talent. Even when the feedback is aimed at addressing performance issues, the authentic compassionate leader delivers it in such a manner that the followers who receive the feedback feel understood, respected, and heard and do not feel like it was a personal attack on him or her. Authentic compassionate leaders also encourage conversations that facilitate change through the relational aspects of leadership. Their manner of communication is inclusive and does not involve making demands or not talking at those they lead and, in fact, facilitate dialogue and conversations that are of value to each stakeholder and which, in turn, encourages and promotes engagement and commitment. This is Tenet One.

- **Open and Transparent**

As an authentic compassionate leader, you understand that being human at times involves making mis-steps or errors. In fact, leaders that are authentic including transparent and capable of sharing their mis-steps are the ones followers are more comfortable approaching and relating to as they feel more human. Many leaders in the business world are unforgiving of themselves when they make a mis-step, or they may feel the same by stakeholders. The simple truth is that although some errors can be costly, we are all human and, as such, prone to mis-steps. Compassionate leaders accept this as a fact of business and life. This, of course, does not exclude consequences or the accountability for poor judgment and behavior. A compassionate leader, however, considers mis-steps as opportunities to learn and develop from without feeling the need to not forgive themselves for them. Typically, leaders who aspire to unattainable or unrealistic goals are more prone to judging themselves and anyone else who is unable to meet up with their unrealistic expectations. Such leaders also tend to cover up their mis-steps or misrepresent the fact.

- **Authentic and Genuine**

Compassionate leaders are authentic and value-based; they are authentic compassionate leaders. Their followers find out there is never a need to question the motives of any leader's behaviors or decisions. The followers are also aware that they are made with the greater good in mind and not self-serving leadership behavior that is known to be pervasive in traditional and corporate management cultures.

- **Committed and Courageous**

Because compassion is infrequent in the business world, compassionate leaders display a distinct level of courage when they choose to be compassionate to themselves or others. After all, they are working against the status quo and more than likely challenging the typical management status quo and expectations of how a leader should behave or how to be a leader. They possess a sense of responsibility and duty to do the right thing, to act ethically, and to assess the impact of behaviors and decisions on everyone that may be affected by them.

Authentic Compassionate Leadership

The principal ingredients to a successful, effective leaderare authenticity and compassion. Many see authenticity and compassion as signs of weakness and being soft; however, true authenticity and compassion are the characteristics that are needed to convert knowledge into wisdom. As a wise leader, one of the tools that you can use to perceive the needs of those you lead is compassion. It allows you to astutely determine a course of action that would be of the greatest benefit to both the team and the individual as well as the institution or organization and our higher vision or 'why'.

Leadership is about being a leader. Showing our selves and working with followers with authenticity and compassion. The noblest and the highest form of leadership can only be realized when authenticity and compassion are the primary operating elements.

The Three Tenets

Tenet One: Value for Who You Are

Tenet Two: Making a Positive Difference

Tenet Three: Continuing to Grow

Printed in Great Britain
by Amazon